Fidos and Fifth-Graders

Nancy Oblak Moore

Fidos and Fifth-Graders

Tate Publishing & *Enterprises*

Fidos and Fifth Graders
Copyright © 2011 by Nancy Oblak Moore. All rights reserved.

No part of this publication may be reproduced, stored in a retrieval system or transmitted in any way by any means, electronic, mechanical, photocopy, recording or otherwise without the prior permission of the author except as provided by USA copyright law.

Scripture quotations are taken from the Holy Bible, *King James Version*, Cambridge, 1769. Used by permission. All rights reserved.

This novel is a work of fiction. However, several names, descriptions, entities, and incidents included in the story are based on the lives of real people.

The opinions expressed by the author are not necessarily those of Tate Publishing, LLC.

Published by Tate Publishing & Enterprises, LLC
127 E. Trade Center Terrace | Mustang, Oklahoma 73064 USA
1.888.361.9473 | www.tatepublishing.com

Tate Publishing is committed to excellence in the publishing industry. The company reflects the philosophy established by the founders, based on Psalm 68:11,
"The Lord gave the word and great was the company of those who published it."

Book design copyright © 2011 by Tate Publishing, LLC. All rights reserved.
Cover design by Shawn Collins
Interior design by Joel Uber

Published in the United States of America

ISBN: 978-1-61346-323-9
1. Biography & Autobiography: Educators
2. Pets: Dogs, General
11.07.29

To Dad, Mom, and Sally

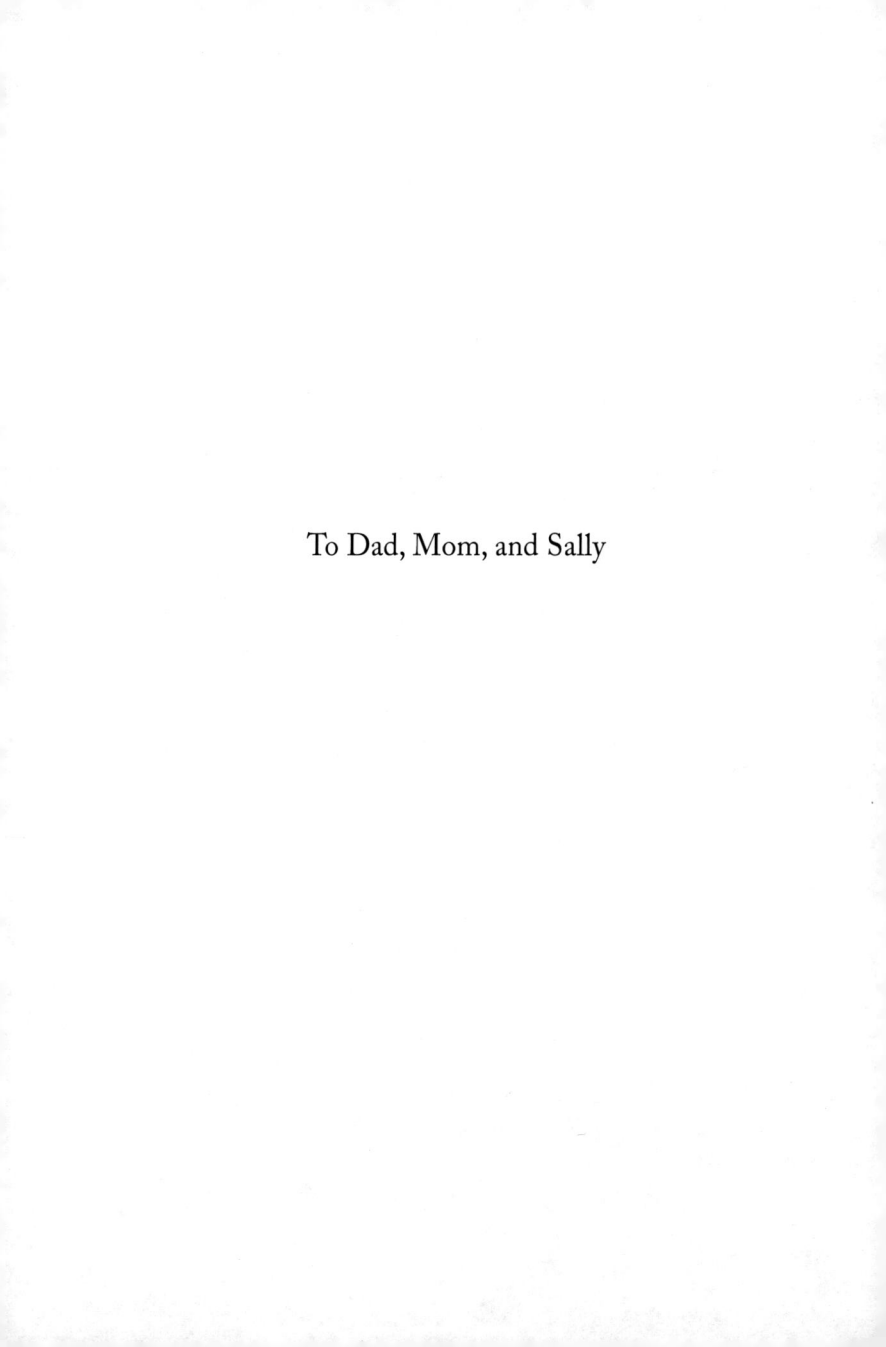

Acknowledgments

Thank you to the Kanawha Charleston Humane Society, Charleston, West Virginia, for providing a safe, if only temporary, haven for our furry friends.

Thank you to Walton Elementary/Middle School for giving me the opportunity to have a career that I can still smile about after thirty-one years of teaching.

Thank you to Alison for dedicating her life toward maintaining and improving the health of our pets.

Table of Contents

13	Introduction
15	Driveway Dogs
19	Day One
23	Tippy
31	Comin' Around
35	The Mentor
39	What's Expected?
43	Routine
45	The Littlest People

51	Good Mail
53	Mommy's Hat
61	Persistence
67	No Dog of Mine
73	Commands
77	Statistics
81	Stories
85	Keep Smiling
89	For Karen
93	Weather or Not
97	Shortcuts
101	Yes, Toni?
107	Labels
111	Hey!
113	Basic Needs
119	Quiet Little Girls
121	Rewards
127	The Artist
131	Abandoned

135	"The"
139	Drivin' It Home
143	Grand Old Stories
147	Balls of Fur
151	Rules
155	Labels
159	Fidos and Fifth Graders
165	Bombs Away!
171	Paw Prints on My Back
173	Fake It, Freddy
175	Make Your Own Fun
179	They Can!

Introduction

After ten years of being a sixth grade classroom teacher in an elementary school and three years of being the junior high science teacher in a seventh through twelfth grade secondary school, I had the opportunity of being a fifth grade teacher at the new middle school. I jumped at the chance to teach fifth grade. I had always heard that it was the ideal grade to teach. The students usually have mastered their basic skills well enough that a teacher can actually "do" something with the children. The average ten- to eleven-year-old is sensitive, concerned about environmental and social issues, and is willing and eager to get involved. The typical fifth grader is beginning to become independent but is still open, responsive, and dependent upon his teacher for support, encouragement, conversation, and affection. And I found in my year with the fifth graders that most of them have an avid love of dogs, a love that I recently rediscovered in myself after living "petless" for twenty-six years.

Driveway Dogs

> And God said, *Let the earth bring forth the living creature after his kind, cattle, and creeping thing, and beast of the earth after his kind:* and it was so. And God made the beast of the earth after his kind, and cattle after their kind, and every thing that creepeth upon the earth after his kind: and God saw that it was good.
>
> Genesis 1:24-25

Normally, my trip home from school is via the main state road, Route 119 South and Interstate 79

South. One afternoon I had to pick up some newspapers for recycling at the home of one of my students. I hurriedly left the middle school in order to get down the road before the buses exited the elementary school. I turned up the hollow on the narrow secondary road that would lead me to my student's home. As I followed the road that followed the creek which had carved the valley eons ago, I noticed dogs sitting in driveways near the edge of the secondary road. The dogs were too numerous to be coincidental; every third or fourth driveway had a dog or two, sitting tall, with ears cocked forward. Most of the dogs were large mutts, shaggy furry mongrels, dogs whose ancestry may be difficult to trace. What were they doing?

After picking up the newspapers and heading back down the hollow, I discovered the answer to my question. I stopped when I saw the red blinking lights of the school bus approaching me. The bus stopped directly in front of a driveway with a sitting dog. The dog stood up. Three children spilled out of the bus and scurried across the road to the awaiting dog. The dog bounced and leaped and returned the children's hugs with wet tongue kisses. As I watched, the three children bounded home, accompanied by their tail-wagging companion. As I continued toward home, I saw that the driveways were now empty. The dogs had done their duty and had gone home.

Johnny may have had a bad day at school. Teacher may have scolded him; he may have failed a test. Perhaps Mom will be too busy to hug him when he comes in the door. But how fortunate for him that he is met each day with the unconditional love of his dog.

Prayer:
Our Heavenly Father, We thank you for the creation of animals which serve us in so many ways. Amen.

Day One

> Bear ye one another's burdens, and so fulfil
> the law of Christ.
>
> Galatians 6:2

Today was the first day of school. I was the new fifth grade teacher. I led my new little charges through their first day at the middle school. We toured the building, found our lockers, and changed classes, teachers, and books. I walked the children to lunch, to recess, to the restroom. The students were polite, receptive, and responsive, but I also noticed that a few of them were quite disorganized, dropping papers here, forgetting a book there. Two little boys in particular seemed to be having problems.

Finally, at three o'clock, the bell rang to dismiss the students for the day. The other fifth grade teacher was going to lead all our students to the buses, so I hung back to check the hallways to see if we had missed anyone.

There, lumbering toward the outside steps (the fire escape route), was one of the disorganized boys I mentioned earlier. In his arms he had every textbook he had been given that day.

"To show my mother," he said.

I didn't know his name. I didn't even know if he was in my homeroom. But I knew he would have to take the outside steps if he wanted to catch his bus in time, and I knew he wasn't going to make it alone. I followed him, picking up books and papers as they fell. Was I encouraging his independence or being a mother hen?

"Thanks," he said, as I piled the dropped items back on top of his stack.

With his little shoulders squared and his arms stretched straight with his heavy load, he turned toward the bus, his determined yet calm little face leading his plodding feet forward.

I know that first day of school was stressful and tiring for me; it was probably overwhelming for most of the children. But as I watched my little fire escape companion stumble up the bus steps, wait for the bus driver to retrieve a book that he had dropped, and finally plop into the seat that would take him home, I sighed with relief.

That little one has the determination and attitudes necessary to make it in this world, I thought. *I just hope Mom is waiting for him at the bus stop!*

Prayer:

Dear Lord, With your help we will face new situations and problems with strength and determination. Amen.

And God said, *Let Us make man in Our image, after Our likeness: and let them have dominion over the fish of the sea, and over the fowl of the air, and over the cattle, and over all the earth, and over every creeping thing that creepeth over the earth*

Genesis 1:26

"We need to talk about something," my husband, Dan, said to me one Saturday afternoon in February a year ago.

My daughter, Alison, was spending the day at a friend's house, and Dan sounded serious, so I put aside my work to listen.

"What?" I asked.

"I found a dog. A puppy, I mean," he said.

"Where?"

"Along the road to our land," he said.

"And?"

"And I picked him up. It's so cold outside."

"Where is he now?" I asked.

I was alarmed, as we were not permitted to have dogs or cats in the trailer park where we lived.

"He's out on the land," Dan said, referring to three acres of woodland we had recently purchased on which to build our home.

"Running loose?" I asked.

"No, I put him in the tool shed."

I looked at my watch: four thirty.

"You know we can't handle a dog at this time. He couldn't stay outside overnight in this cold. And you know we aren't allowed dogs at the trailer. I'll call the pound."

I found out from the worker at the humane society that we had until six o'clock to bring the dog in. Dan stood and stared at his shoes as I talked on the phone. I rushed him out to the car, and we raced down the hollow leading to our land.

"Hurry now," I said, as I pulled up in front of the toolshed.

Dan returned to the car with a pink blanket concealing a squirming load. He sat down, put his load on the floor of the car at his feet, and peeled the blanket away. A black nose with pink spots poked out at me.

Dan apologized for the appearance of the nose.

"He'll lose those pink spots," he said.

The puppy that followed the nose out of the blanket was a tricolor, mostly white. He blinked up at me.

Don't get attached, I told myself.

The puppy crawled up onto Dan's lap. I proceeded toward the pound.

"What kind of dog do you think he is?" Dan asked.

"I don't know anything about dogs," I grumbled. "He looks like he has some hunter in him, maybe beagle or foxhound?"

"Look at the size of those feet," Dan said.

The paws were humongous. I reached out to touch one; the puppy licked my hand. Steering the car with one hand, I rubbed behind his ears with the other. He pointed his snout skyward in dog ecstasy.

We reached the pound in time. Dan reported where and when he had found the puppy while I strolled around. I had never visited a pound before. As a child in southwestern Pennsylvania, I had received all my kittens and puppies from local farmers whose animals had just had litters. I timidly entered the first two dog runs. One dog barked, and eventually all dogs barked; the noise was discomforting and deafening. As I walked by, the dogs ran up to the door of their pens. Most would rise up on their hind legs, press their snout through the wire mesh, and wiggle, wag, and whine for attention.

Don't get attached, I told myself.

After leaving kennels A and B, I entered the other half of the pound—kennels C and D. Many of the dogs were mutts, but I was surprised at the number of purebred and nearly purebred dogs residing at the establishment: cocker spaniels, Airedales, and English sheepdogs.

I made my way down to where Dan and one of the pound workers were standing. Dan's little buddy, the tricolor puppy, was sitting straight and tall in pen C-5. A cocker spaniel was chewing at his ear.

"How long do you keep them?" I asked the worker.

"Five days for dogs, longer if we have room and the dog has a good disposition," she said.

The puppy's brown eyes were difficult to see in his brown mask of fur, but his shifting tan eyebrows gave away the fact that he was looking from me, to David, to the pound worker, and back again to me.

"Good luck, boy," I said.

Dan blew his nose.

I know; we're just old softies. Monday afternoon Dan surprised our daughter with a pillowcase which, when opened, revealed a pink-and-black nose with a tricolor puppy attached. The pillowcase served as Tippy's vehicle into and out of our trailer. The "bag of laundry" grew fuller and deeper, and eventually the pillowcase was replaced with a full-sized laundry bag to carry the now forty-five-pound load.

"Is Tippy a bad secret?" asked my daughter, Alison.

"I don't think so, honey. It will just be for a short time—time this little guy wouldn't have had otherwise."

Tippy filled some missing links in our family. For Alison, he was a friend that never turned on her and was an endless supply of unconditional love. For Dan, until the weather warmed up sufficiently for the dog to spend the days in his pen on the land, Tippy was his constant companion in his exterminating business. The "bug man" became known as the "dog man," and to see the pair of them coming down the road—Dan driving and Tippy sitting tall in the passenger seat of the truck—was a comical sight. For me, Tippy served as a release from the pressures of the classroom, and we would wrestle and play as robustly as we dared in our small home. For the entire family,

Tippy served as a common interest that drew us together even closer than ever.

Prayer:

Dear God, Man has domesticated animals that have served him well since pre-history. Now, through careless management, we are exterminating millions of dogs and cats each year. Please help us to be responsible pet owners and reduce the pet population to help eliminate the senseless slaughter. Amen.

Comin' Around

*For I the Lord thy God will hold thy right hand,
saying unto thee, fear not; I will help thee.*
                              Isaiah 41:13

When our high school became a middle school, many changes occurred. The transfer of half of our teachers to the new consolidated high school split up colleagues who had worked together for decades. Most of the teachers who remained at the middle school were not used to dealing with middle-grade children and their hyperactivity, their short attention spans, and their dependence upon their teachers. Lessons had to involve the younger student more actively; lectures no longer sufficed.

The principal, Mr. Carpenter, admitted to us teachers at a meeting before the start of the school year that he was a bit anxious, as he didn't know what to expect from students in the middle grades.

Don't worry, boss, I thought. *I've been working with this age children for fourteen years, and they still surprise me every day!*

Mr. Carpenter had been comfortable as a high school principal at his old alma mater, his pride and joy. He had been a classmate of the parents of many of the students and had a good rapport with the high-school-age student. But the name of the school changed; the age of the students had diminished, and the face that I saw in front of the office was not always happy as it towered over the mass of youngsters scurrying to get to the right class at the right time. I was concerned.

After the fifth graders finished lunch and recess each day, we would return to our classroom, while the older students had their break. Our afternoon reading lesson was, on pretty days, usually accompanied by the sound of the seventh and eighth graders outside at play.

One day in November, I heard a deep, strong voice in the midst of the children's voices. This deep voice was not giving orders or directions—it was joining in the play. Who was this? The raised eyebrows of my students told me that they were curious too. I walked to our second-story window and looked down at the school driveway. There, standing in a circle of children, was the principal, in dress pants, shirt, and tie, clapping his hands and looking like a big kid. The same big guy who could jive so effectively with the high school crowd was beginning to find himself among the middle school children. My students clustered around me to watch.

As I eventually shooed them back to their desks, Marty said, "Mr. Carpenter needs to tuck in his shirt!"

The children and I giggled as I thought, *Leave him alone today, kids. He's comin' around, comin' around...*

Prayer:

Dear Lord, When we face the changes and unexpected occurrences that challenge us today, let us not do it alone. Amen.

The Mentor

Weeping may endure for a night, but joy cometh in the morning.

Psalms 30:5b

I was to be Tom's mentor. Tom was taking over the seventh and eighth grade science position that I had recently vacated, so I was the likely choice of teachers to "show him the ropes." As a mentor, I was ready with support and suggestions, but since what works for me in the classroom may not necessarily work for another teacher, the mentoring process has no guarantees.

When I met Tom at the get-acquainted meeting, I learned of his recent divorce and of his young son that he missed dearly. I remembered the hours of preparation I had put in each night when I had had Tom's position of science teacher. I remembered my first year of teaching and how overwhelming the work load had been. My heart went out to this young man, along with a prayer or two.

After we finished lunch at the get-acquainted meeting, Tom excused himself.

"Got to check on my dog," he said.

"Your what?" I said, but he was already out of earshot. I watched through the plate glass window as Tom walked up to a truck on the parking lot. He let down the tailgate, untied a rope, and out jumped a black Labrador retriever. The dog wiggled and pranced and licked his greetings all over Tom's face. I knew from this point on that Tom would survive. No matter what the demands of his job may be, he would be greeted every evening by a mass of black fur and pink tongue who would jump on him, wag its tail, and smother him with love. How could he lose?

Prayer:

Dear Lord, Be with us in times of loneliness and need. Amen.

What's Expected?

For I know the thoughts that I think toward you, saith the Lord, *thoughts of peace*, and not of evil, *to give you an expected end.*
                                    Jeremiah 29:11

One of the most wonderful aspects of moving from the junior high to the fifth grade was that the fifth graders would freely and openly respond to their teacher. Friends are important to this age group, but the teacher is still a very "significant other" to a fifth grader.

I, as a junior high teacher, would always close every class with, "Have a good day." I got used to the fact that I would get no overt class response, maybe just a quiet "good-bye" or two from individual students as they walked by.

When the bell rang at the end of the day with fifth graders, a chorus of farewells would ring out, "Good-bye, Mrs. Moore! Good-bye, Mrs. Moore! Good-bye, Mrs. Moore!" If I would be the first to say "Good-bye!" the class would respond in unison, "Good-bye, Mrs. Moore!"

I loved it!

I discussed this characteristic of the middle-grade child with my husband at dinnertime.

"The change seems to happen over the summer between sixth grade and seventh grade. It's amazing!"

My daughter, Alison, then a fourth grader, listened as she ate.

The next evening Alison sat down on the couch beside me. She folded her arms in front of her and frowned.

"Now, Mom, at what age do kids stop talking to their teacher?" she asked.

Oh, no, I thought, *What had I done?* Alison has always loved school and adored her teachers. She felt her teachers can do no wrong. In fact, if I said one thing and the teacher said something else, the teacher was always right in Alison's eyes. I didn't want to do anything to change her love and respect for her teachers.

"Oh, that happens with some kids, but others are friendly to their teachers all the way through college," I said.

Alison seemed to accept what I said. I was more careful after that what I discussed about the middle-grade child in front of her. Children often behave in the way we expect them to act. If we expect them to be trouble, they often are. If we accept them with "clean slates" at the beginning of the school year, we are often pleasantly surprised with the positive changes in their behavior and attitude.

No, Alison, it is not expected. It just happens, for better or for worse, as children grow toward independence.

Prayer:

Dear Lord, Help us to appreciate the good in children, no matter what age or stage they are in. Amen.

Routine

> Let your light so shine before men, that they may see your good works, and glorify your Father which is in heaven.
>
> Matthew 5:16

According to my husband and daughter, Tippy's behavior changes around three forty in the afternoon each weekday. He stops playing; he stays away from the food and water. He lies on the floor with his head on his front legs, his eyes open. And he listens. At the sound of a motor vehicle, he raises his head, ears cocked forward, head tilted to one side. When the vehicle passes, Tippy puts his head back on his front legs, listens, and waits. He repeats this routine until he hears my car pull into the driveway at approximately four fifteen, and, at this point, he jumps to his feet, runs to the door, and waits with tail wagging for "Mommy" to appear. "Mommy" means a pat on the head, some additional bustle and noise, but more importantly, "Mommy" means dinner!

Tippy shows signs of anxiety when "Mommy's" late and the routine is changed. He actually paces the floor when Alison and I go out of town overnight, and he goes from room to room in the trailer looking for us.

Children need predictability in their lives also. Surprises may be the spices of life, but routine is the meat and potatoes, the substance upon which our lives are based, the source of our safety and security.

Prayer:

Our Heavenly Father, In our sometimes helter-skelter lives of today, help us to work from a routine for our peace of mind and for that of our children. And Lord, please be part of our routine daily. Amen.

The Littlest People

> Better is a little with righteousness than great revenues without right.
>
> Proverbs 16:8

Did you ever notice how the littlest people (in body size) are sometimes the hardest workers? Perhaps they feel that they must overcompensate to make up for their lack of physical stature.

A local radio station announced a newspaper recycling drive. The three schools that brought in the most newspapers by weight were to win cash prizes. I didn't think a tiny rural school such as ours would have much chance at winning one of the prizes, but since I usually get a recycling effort started at some point every school year, I thought this was a good enough time to start.

My fifth graders went all out on the effort. The school year was young, and these littlest members of the middle school were eager to impress their teacher. If she wanted newspapers, then newspapers were what she was going to get!

The first day of the newspaper drive, Jill's dad dropped off a pickup truck load of newspapers at the school. That afternoon, Angie's mom brought a full Blazer.

"Mrs. Moore, my grandma has a whole lot of newspapers, but I don't know how to get them to school," said Lisa, the tiniest girl in the class.

"Ask your grandma if I can pick them up on my way home from school tomorrow," I said.

Tuesday afternoon found me following Lisa's bus to her grandmother's house. Lisa hopped off the bus and raced into the house to get Grandma as I parked my car.

After Grandma and I had been properly introduced, she and Lisa led me to the building where the newspapers were stored. The papers were neatly packed in brown grocery bags. Lisa picked one up.

"Gee, Lisa, that bag's almost as big as you! Let me carry it," I said.

"No, I've got it, Mrs. Moore," Lisa said, and headed toward my car.

Grandma leaned down, supported by her cane, and picked up a bag.

"Oh, no, let me get them!" I said, but Grandma just smiled and carefully maneuvered herself toward my car.

Obviously these two little ladies were going to help me whether I wanted their help or not, so I grabbed two bags and went huffing and puffing off to my car.

We must have made ten trips each back and forth from the building to my car. My Subaru hatchback was loaded to the point that I had to use my side mirrors to see what was behind me. As I sank wearily into the driver's seat, I waved to Lisa and her grandma who were standing on the porch, smiling at me.

The next morning, Tommy and Brian each brought in an armload of newspapers.

"We went up and down the road with my wagon to get these." Tommy beamed.

"Well, bless your hearts," I said.

"My neighbor has a bunch more if you can pick them up tonight," said Brian.

So Wednesday afternoon found me following Brian's bus up the hollow. Brian emerged from his neighbor's house with the equivalence of about three Sunday papers, but it was quite an armload for the little guy.

"Do you think we'll win?" Brian asked as he loaded the papers in my car.

"I don't know," I said, "but anyone who recycles is a winner."

I didn't have much hope of winning any prize money in the contest. Our little school of 230 students did not stand much of a chance against the large high schools in the Kanawha Valley with enrollments close to one thousand.

I had gone home every day that week, Monday through Thursday, with my little car crammed full of newspapers, which my husband put in a storage building.

"You'd better take my truck on Friday," Dan said.

Friday was the last day of the paper drive. Not only did I need Dan's truck, which we stuffed full with newspapers, but a fellow teacher filled his truck bed with the remaining newspapers and followed me to the drop-off point in Charleston. I don't know if I was exceeding the weight limit of my husband's truck, but I do know that both trucks rode rather low on their tires as our little caravan slowly made its way to the state capital.

When all of our newspapers were weighed in, we were about six pounds short of two tons of paper. When the radio station called us Monday morning and told us we had won second place and $250, we were ecstatic.

I guess a "little" effort does go a long way.

Prayer:
Dear Lord, May we be judged in this life by our efforts and not by our stature. Amen.

Good Mail

> While we look not at the things which are
> seen, but at the things which are not seen:
> for the things which are seen are temporal;
> but the things which are not seen are eternal.
> 2 Corinthians 4:18

I came home after a day of teaching the fifth grade, and my husband greeted me with, "You got some good mail today."

Oh, boy, I thought. *Maybe a check had come in. Maybe a grant I had requested had been funded,* I thought, as I walked over to the table where we put our daily mail. There, on top of the usual stack of bills and advertisements, were two letters from former students of mine. I tore into the letters, which were filled with news about the new high school both students were attending as freshmen this year, the new friends they were making, the classes they were taking, and the extracurricular activities they were getting involved in. Both students appeared to be so happy and excited about their school experience. Were these the same students who last year were fearful and apprehensive about starting in at the new consolidated high school?

As I settled back on the couch with that contented mellow feeling I always get after hearing from one of my "old kids," I thought, *You were right, Dan. That was some good mail.*

Prayer:
Our Heavenly Father, Help us to remember that people are much more important than things. Amen.

Mommy's Hat

> To every thing there is a season, and a time
> to every purpose under the heaven:
> Ecclesiastes 3:1

When Tippy was still a young pup, he would bark if we left him in the car. As soon as he realized he was being left behind, he would start barking. If we were going to a restaurant, we would sit near a window so we could watch him bark throughout our meal. We could see his efforts, his mouth opening and closing, his body and head jerking, but we couldn't hear the resulting sound. He would stop barking as soon as we got back into the car.

Once we left him tied outside at my mother's house while we celebrated my sister's birthday inside, and Tippy barked for two hours straight.

Eventually Tippy realized that we always came back to him whether he barked or not, so he wisely chose to give up the barking.

"If we give him too much attention when he barks, he'll bark all the time," I said.

Sometimes children will misbehave just to get attention. If we as parents and teachers only notice our children when they are doing wrong and only give them "negative attention," they may misbehave more in order to get the attention they want and need so badly.

"I figure a dog will use 'negative attention' to his advantage also, once he figures out how it works. Watch how you react when Tippy does something wrong," I said to my family.

"Guess what Tippy did today," my husband, Dan, said a few days later. "He honked my horn."

"He what?" I said.

"Actually, he put his front paws on the steering wheel and just sort of leaned there…" Dan said.

"For how long?" I asked.

"Oh, about five minutes, I guess. I was servicing the restaurant down the street, and Tippy was waiting for me in the truck. I at first thought someone's horn got stuck. The customers eventually started looking around and getting annoyed. A big man finally walked outside to check it out. Came back in and said, 'Some dumb dog out there's leaning on the horn in that green truck.' Well, I ran out the side door, and there was Tippy, honking and panting with a smile on his face. I don't really think he knew he was making the noise."

I covered my smile.

"How did you react?"

Dan said, "I took him off the horn and said, '*No! Off!*' and he hung his head. I don't think he will do it again."

"I certainly hope not," I said. "I can see the headlines now: Horn-Honking Hound Held For Disturbing Peace."

Tippy never honked again.

Tippy had taken a fancy to a refrigerator magnet of mine. This particular magnet was a miniature little old lady style hat, made of china blue calico and adorned with lace, satin ribbons, and little white silk flowers. One day when I came home from school, I found the hat on the floor. The hat was a bit soggy and disheveled.

"What happened to my hat?" I asked, as I bent to pick it up.

Dan looked up.

"I don't know. Alison, do you know what happened to Mommy's hat?"

"Maybe Tippy had it. I don't know," she said. "Oh!"

I gasped and took the hat over to where Tippy was snoozing on the living room floor.

"What did zu do to Mommy's hat?" I asked.

I knew it was fruitless to scold him now, as he might have committed the crime an hour or two ago, so I teased him instead. He rolled over on his back and exposed his belly in complete trust.

"Don't zu touch Mommy's hat," I taunted, wagging the hat in his face while I rubbed his belly. I put the hat back on the refrigerator.

Daily thereafter, when I came home from work, my hat would be anywhere but on the refrigerator. Its location became a game.

"Where's Mommy's hat?" I would say, as Tippy went into his playful stance. He would follow me as I searched the house. Sometimes the hat, each day a little worse for the wear, would be in plain view in the middle of the living room floor; sometimes it would be under an end table, and once it was in the plastic bucket where we keep Tippy's toys.

"What does this mean?" I asked, shaking the hat in his face. "Is this now Tippy's hat?"

The dog pranced playfully and tried to nip the hat out of my hands.

If I really cared about the hat, the ending of this story may have been different. And Tippy is good about not touching anything of ours (except the hat). Nevertheless, one day I came home to a small soggy clutch of white silk flowers in the center of the living room rug. Tippy, lying nearby, watched my every move as I picked up the flowers.

"What did zu do?" I asked him quietly, holding up the flowers.

He sneezed and pranced.

I threw the flowers away and, after finding the hat in the bedroom, I hung it back on the refrigerator.

"You leave Mommy's hat alone," I warned.

Tippy chased his tail and went into his play bow. I wrestled him to the ground and tickled his ribs.

The next evening the satin ribbon was being guarded in the center of the rug by the old tricolor hat chewer. I found the hat and replaced it on the refrigerator door.

"Mommy's hat," I warned.

The following evening there was lace in Tippy's toy bucket.

"Why does he pick on that hat?" asked Dan. "That refrigerator is covered with things, but he only goes after that hat."

"It's a game we play," I said.

When I came home the next day and saw a little pile of white stuffing and a chewed cardboard circle, I knew that the game was over. As I examined the shredded china blue calico that was lying under the kitchen table, I knew that Mommy's hat had seen its last day as a refrigerator magnet. I tossed the remnants in the wastebasket.

Tippy remembered our game the next winter when, as I was driving my car, he chomped on the brim of my new brown felt hat.

"No! Enough!" I ordered. I said nothing about "Mommy's hat," and my tone of voice told Tippy that this hat was not to be played with. But someday, in years to come, when I'm a little older lady and he's a very old dog, I think I'm going to make me a china blue calico hat, complete with lace, ribbons, and flowers, and we'll see what happens.

Prayer:
Dear Lord, Let every day have a laugh, a good memory, and a happy story. Amen.

Persistence

Ask, and it shall be given you; seek, and you shall find; knock, and it shall be opened unto you: for he that asketh, receiveth; *and he that seeketh, findeth; and to him that knocketh it shall be opened.*

Matthew 7:7-8

Persistence is a quality that I have noticed in quite a few fifth graders. These youngest members of the middle school clan sometimes take on tasks that would overwhelm others of greater age and size. This is the story of Treena:

A few weeks before Christmas, I introduced an assignment to my language arts classes. The students were to write a seven to nine hundred word story to enter into a writing contest. The stories would be due the first day of school in January. I reviewed the steps in the art of writing a story, and we discussed the theme dictated by the contest rules.

"Can we start now?" asked Treena.

"You mean writing? Well, sure. Get your journals, and find a comfortable place to write," I said. I thought that the students would need more time to think about the assignment, maybe "sleep on it." But they were ready, and I was willing to let them use the remaining twenty minutes of class to write.

When the bell rang to dismiss class, I reminded the students, "Stories are due the day after Christmas vacation. You've got about three weeks. Class dismissed."

The next morning Treena came bouncing into my classroom.

"May I share my story today, Mrs. Moore?" she asked.

"What story?" I said.

"My story for the contest," she said.

"Oh, did you get started with it?" I said.

"No, I got done!" Treena said. "Seven hundred eighty-eight words!"

"My goodness! How long did you work on it?" I asked.

"About three hours yesterday evening," she said. She handed me five pages of notebook paper filled with the words of her story. "Will you keep this until language arts class?" she asked.

"Sure," I said. As she skipped back to her seat, I called, "Good work, Treena."

As I leafed through the story, I shook my head with wonder. I thought of how often I wished I had the energy at the end of a school day to write. I thought of how it would probably take me a week of evenings to write a story of this size. I immediately dug out a folder, labeled it *Contest Stories*, placed Treena's story in the folder, and put the folder in a safe place. I certainly didn't want to lose her work.

That afternoon Treena shared her story with the class. We applauded her efforts. I asked the class to describe the emotions Treena's story made them feel. I asked them to tell of particular words, phrases, or parts of the story that they liked. Finally, I asked them what they might change if they were writing Treena's story. Treena wrote notes to herself in the margins of her paper.

"Treena's next job will be to consider our suggestions and revise her story," I said. "Then she can share it with us again."

I expected to hear from Treena in about a week, but the next morning she skipped up to me again.

"May I share this in language arts?" she asked.

"What is this?" I asked.

"My second draft," she said.

"Wonderful!" I said, and tucked the story away in the folder.

When Treena shared her second draft in language arts class, I expected a few minor changes, but she had actually rewritten the entire story and had made major revisions. We applauded her efforts. We told her what we liked, and we suggested changes she could possibly make. Treena took notes.

The next morning I stood at the front of my classroom with my hands on my hips, my lips in a tight little grin, and my eyes on the door. When Treena skipped in, I nodded my head, tapped my foot, and held out my hand.

"Third draft," she called, as she slapped her story into my hand and skipped away.

My foot kept tapping, but my head shook from side to side.

"That kid is amazing," I said.

Treena continued with her revisions, and only one night in the next two weeks did she fail to work on her story.

"We went Christmas shopping last night. I'm sorry, Mrs. Moore," she said.

I threw up my hands, shook my head, and smiled. "You've done so much already," I said. "You deserve a break."

Treena was a good model for my other students. More and more students brought in their first drafts and revisions to share. I believe that Treena's persistence did more than I as a teacher could ever do to inspire the students to write and to encourage them to share their writing with us.

With all her efforts, Treena finally turned out a fair little story. Her story didn't win in the contest, but she was definitely a winner to me.

Prayer:

Dear God, Let the little ones never lose their persistence and drive toward constructive things. Amen.

No Dog of Mine

Thou, even thou, art Lord alone; thou hast made heaven, the heaven of heavens, with their entire host, the earth, and all things that are therein, the seas, and all that is therein, and thou preservest them all; and the host of heaven worshippeth thee.

Nehemiah 9:6

When we first found Tippy, I was finishing up my last year as the junior high science teacher. My eighth graders and I were discussing animal training and behavior.

"What are you teaching your dog to do?" asked Sam.

"So far, he will come when called. He knows his name, and he will give me his paw," I said. "I'm trying to get him to talk, but no response yet."

The class chuckled.

"My dog talks," said Allen. Our heads all turned in Allen's direction. "He calls all the people in my family by their name."

"What does he call you, *Ral-run*?" I growled.

The class tittered.

"No, it's not a growl or a bark," said Allen.

"Is it a whine?" I asked.

"No, it's a special voice. A talking voice," said Allen. "He says 'Mom' and 'Dad' too."

My students and I were pretty amazed at Allen's revelation. We talked of maybe videotaping his dog's performance or visiting Allen for a demonstration.

"No," Allen said. "He won't do it in front of strangers. He gets too excited."

When I went home that evening, I was determined to get Tippy to talk. For about two weeks I had been trying to get him to beg for a dog biscuit by saying, "I'm hungry. I'm hungry." Tippy had danced around and tried to snap the biscuit out of my fingers but did not respond vocally.

"No dog of mine is going to talk," said my husband, as he watched.

I decided to go for the big guns. I opened the refrigerator, cut off a chunk of ham, and sliced it into smaller pieces. I held one of the pieces of ham in front of Tippy's face and said, "I'm hungry. I'm hungry." Tippy pranced.

"I'm hungry. I'm hungry," I said.

Tippy went into his play bow and barked.

"No!" I said. "I'm hungry. I'm hungry."

I repeated this routine until Tippy made a sound like I'd never heard him make before.

"Uhhh," he said.

"*Good boy!*" I said. His head jerked back, and he blinked with surprise. I popped the ham into his awaiting mouth.

"What did he say?" asked my daughter.

"I don't know, but it sounded like he was trying to talk," I said. "We have to reward his initial efforts so he knows what we want him to do.

Then, the closer he gets to the sounds we want, the greater his reward."

I rewarded Tippy's "Uhhh" for an evening or two. He would see the ham and say, "Uhhh" with little or no prompting. I thought it was time to expect more.

"I'm hungry," I said, dangling the ham in front of his nose.

"Uhhh," he said.

"No, I'm hungry," I said, slowly and emphatically.

"Uhhh," he said.

"No, I'm hungry," I said.

Tippy pranced around, sneezed, went down on his belly, sneezed again, and said, "Uhh, uhh, uhh."

"*Good boy!*" I shrieked.

Tippy's whole body jerked. His front paws left the floor for a split second. He gobbled his ham as I stroked his head.

"What did he do?" asked Alison.

"Three syllables," I said.

Now Tippy would only get his ham if he uttered three syllables. It amused me that he always danced around and sneezed three or four times before he would say his three syllables.

Within a week's time, I could hear the correct vowel sounds.

"Uhh-uhh-ee," Tippy would say.

That's as close to "I'm hungry" that Tippy has come. Since I had usually done our little talking exercises at eight o'clock, Tippy now comes up to me every evening around that time, prances, sneezes, and tells me, "Uhh-uhh-ee."

Prayer:
Our Heavenly Father, There is no end to the wonders of your little creations. Amen.

Commands

Train up a child in the way he should go: and when he is old, he will not depart from it.
Proverbs 22:6

When training dogs, your orders and commands should be short, firm, and consistent. Our dog, was quick to learn and eager to please. I had vowed not to punish him with anything worse than the word "*No!*," and rewards (bologna and hot dogs) worked so well with him that I seldom ever had to respond negatively.

Without realizing it, initially, my short commands found their way into my classroom.

"Sit!" I barked to anyone who had drifted out of his seat.

"Stay!" I ordered to the line leader when I didn't want him following me yet.

"Come!" I called to the student whom I needed at my desk, and "Enough!" I hollered when my class got too rowdy.

The students were amused and pointed out my behavior to me. I took it a step further and occasionally complimented with "Good girl" or "Good boy" and an accompanying pat on the student's head.

My commands did not work with Bonnie. Bonnie loved to write on the chalkboard. I allowed my students to practice their spelling words on the chalkboard once each week, but any other time the chalkboards were off-limits. Yet often, when I turned around, there would be Bonnie, chalking away.

"Sit, Bonnie," I'd say, then, as Bonnie put the chalk down, I would turn back to the student I had been working with. I'd turn around a minute or two later to see that Bonnie was still at it.

"Sit, Bonnie," I said more sternly than before. She would put the chalk down; I would turn back to my work. This cycle would repeat three or four more times.

"Bonnie!" I finally cried in exasperation. "I can teach my dog to talk, but I can't teach you to sit!"

"I'm not a dog, Mrs. Moore," Bonnie said.

"No, and you aren't sittin', either," I said.

Short, firm, and consistent did not work with Bonnie. A phone call to her mother did, for about a week. Maybe I should have contacted the leader of the pack (the principal) to see if he had any suggestions.

Prayer:

Dear Lord, Free us from the drudgeries of discipline so we will be free to really lead the learners. Amen.

Statistics

> And God shall wipe away all tears from their eyes; and there shall be no more death, neither sorrow, nor crying, neither shall there be any more pain: for the former things are passed away.
>
> Revelation 21:4

I visited the pound today. A family had just dropped off a basket of five puppies, two of which were already too big to put in the puppy pens.

"If we put them in the regular dog runs, they don't stand much of a chance to be adopted," one of the Humane Society officers said.

"One of their dogs had six puppies; the other had seven," said another worker, shaking his head. "If people would just be more responsible with their pets and get them spayed or neutered, or at least pen up their females when they are in heat, we might have a chance at tackling the problem of pet overpopulation."

The statistics from the Kanawha Charleston Humane Association newsletter that I read were shocking. In the first quarter of 1994, 881 dogs and puppies were taken in; 197 were adopted, and 725 were destroyed. The data on cats were equally grim: 611 cats were taken in during the three month period; 93 were adopted, and 476 were destroyed. Charleston, West Virginia, is a relatively small city, its data representing the tip of the iceberg of a massive problem nationwide.

The workers at the pound spent a few minutes petting the puppies and scratching them behind their ears. These loving people are the ones who feed, walk, and otherwise care for the dogs and puppies in the animals' stay at the pound. The workers are also the ones who help in the euthanasia of the dogs when their allowed time is up. How tragic that people who obviously love animals enough to want to work with them have to witness and assist in their destruction!

I left the pound that day with an especially heavy heart. My mind focused on one particular dog—an Airedale mix that, when standing on all fours, was tall enough to almost look me straight in the eye. He was full of love and energy and pranced and danced for me. Who would adopt a dog of that size? He probably weighed 150 pounds or more. He would consume buckets of dog food and, because of his size and energy, would be unsuitable for young children. (And I doubt anyone makes a pillowcase big enough.)

Good-bye, big Airedale. You're probably destined to become another statistic in the ongoing sad story of homeless unwanted pets.

What a waste.

Prayer:

Dear Father, Forgive us for our careless mismanagement of our pets and the resulting destruction of your gentle creatures. Amen.

Stories

> But my God shall supply all your need according to his riches in glory by Christ Jesus.
>
> Philippians 4:19

Shortly before Christmas, a movie aired on television concerning the nation's homeless. Fifth graders are very concerned about social issues and are very sensitive to problems they hear about on television, so I wasn't surprised when the issue of the homeless made its way into the stories my students were writing for language arts class.

Their stories were innocent and naive, most of them involving the students going up to a homeless person and inspiring the person to get a job and to completely turn his life around.

As we responded to the stories, the class and I discussed what could make the stories more realistic.

"It's not safe to go up to a stranger on a street, is it?" I asked.

"Where is the money coming from to provide the food and homes for the people in your story?" Bobbie asked.

"If you're volunteering with the homeless all day every day, when would you go to school? How would you make money?" asked Cindy.

The students revised their stories to make them more realistic. Their story characters had bake sales and donated the proceeds to the organizations that help the homeless. The characters volunteered their free time on the weekends to work in soup kitchens to feed the homeless.

Despite these revisions, I felt like I was leading my students up a dead-end street. Are the soup kitchens and the money drives working? Are they enough to tackle the problems of the homeless? What else is being done today? Have I done enough to prepare the students to be the leaders of tomorrow? My students today are the social workers and voters of the next generation. Will they be knowledgeable and prepared?

At least I have lit the necessary sparks. When they are older and able to do more, hopefully the sparks will still glow.

Prayer:

Dear Lord, Guide us as we try to prepare young people to take on the problems of the world. Let us know what our limitations are and when we need outside help. Amen.

Keep Smiling

These things I have spoken unto you, that in me ye may have peace. In the world ye shall have tribulation: but be of good cheer, I have overcome the world.

John 16:33

"Keep a smile on your face," I whispered to my daughter. "Even if you think you've messed up, keep smiling."

"Okay, Mom," Alison answered, her voice quivering a bit. She took a deep breath and then walked to her starting point.

The music started, and I heard Alison's heels and toes tapping in time with the beat of the song. At age nine, she was competing with junior high and high school girls for a place on the dance team. Alison was a bit anxious that she was considerably younger than the other girls who were auditioning. It didn't help her confidence much when I said, "You've been taking lessons as long as, if not longer than, most of the older girls."

I couldn't see her perform as she tried out for the dance team. But as I listened to her tap shoes moving in time with the music, I was confident that she would at least survive the audition.

Alison had worked daily on her audition number for three weeks in September. Many of the dance steps had to be isolated and practiced over and over until they were executed perfectly, then all the steps had to be put together in the proper order that they came in the routine. It was a lot of hard work.

"Watch the whole thing. I think I've got it," Alison finally said, toward the end of September.

I sat and watched Alison's number from top to bottom. She performed well; her feet did as they should do, and her arms and body moved gracefully.

"Wonderful!" I said. "Now let's put on the finishing touch."

"What do you mean?" she asked.

"The smile. It doesn't matter if your feet and the rest of your body do exactly what they're supposed to do if you don't smile. If you look like you're happy and enjoying yourself, the audience will enjoy your performance. If you look too serious and appear to be concentrating too hard, the audience will worry right along with you. A professional dancer will smile no matter how many times she has done the same dance over and over again and no matter how exhausted she is."

At the audition Alison finally finished her number and sat down to watch the other girls perform. She and the other girls received their score sheets. We were pleased that Alison was one of the eight girls chosen for the team.

A few days later, at the weekly dance class, the teacher took me aside.

"Did you know that Alison's score was third from the top?" she asked.

"No, I had no idea!" I said.

"And do you know why?" the teacher asked. "It was because she smiled. The judge said only three of the girls smiled as they danced, and that was what elevated their scores above those of the other girls."

What did Alison do when I later told her about the reason for her good score? She smiled.

Prayer:
Dear Heavenly Father, Help us to keep smiling. Amen.

For Karen

> For thus saith the Lord GOD, the Holy One of Israel; *In returning and rest shall ye be saved; in quietness and in confidence shall be your strength*: and ye would not.
>
> Isaiah 30:15

Fifth graders seem to need to touch base with their teacher every so often in a day's time. The children seem to appreciate some sort of personal contact with me each period—a look, a word, a touch on the arm. This need was especially evident before seventh period every day. The students were just coming in from recess and were always full of stories to tell me. As I waited for all the students to come into the classroom, a line would form in front of me, each student with something he or she thought important to tell me. I would listen to as many as I could, but when I saw that all students had arrived in the classroom and that some of the seated ones were getting restless, I would announce that it was time to get started with class.

One shy quiet little girl named Karen would immediately sit down and open her book. The other not so shy or quiet little girls would continue to stand in line and try to tell me their tales, until I would have to actually shoo them away. I always made it a point during the class period to find a minute or two for each student who had not had a chance to share with me, but especially for Karen. I remember what it was like to be a quiet child who hid behind her mother's full skirts when she would see her teacher at the grocery store, and who would rather melt away than to contradict an elder. Children like Karen are scarce these days. They need to be encouraged and listened to, for their voice is soft and can be easily overlooked. Karen may have already slipped into the quiet passiveness that so many teenage girls slip into, but if I have anything to do with it, when Karen talks, I'll listen.

Prayer:

Dear Father, Please see that no child is overlooked or pushed aside. Amen.

Weather or Not

> The heavens declare the glory of God; and
> the firmament showeth his handywork.
> Psalms 19:1

Whenever I teach a unit on weather, some natural disaster happens. Maybe these disasters are happening all the time, and we are just more aware of them as we listen to the evening news for the weather forecast; I don't know. Over the years, our weather units were supplemented with news reports on hurricanes Andrew and Hugo, several major California earthquakes, and numerous tornadoes. In fact, we experienced firsthand the effects of a tornado as one touched down in a nearby town and the resulting winds sent everything from pollen to front porches flying through the air.

I remember joking with the principal about this last autumn when I was writing a grant for a school-wide science project. I was requesting a weather station that would be set up on the roof of the school to provide weather data for study, and the project would culminate with a trip for all students to the National Weather Service in Charleston, West Virginia.

"Our study of the weather usually leads to some outstanding occurrence. Are you willing to share in the responsibility?" I asked my boss.

"Go for it," he said, as he cosigned the grant proposal.

In November we received the funding for the weather station. I immediately ordered the necessary equipment.

In December we received funding for the field trips. A few days later, the weather station equipment came in the mail. And shortly after that, the trouble began.

That winter (1993-1994), we had at least four major snowstorms. We missed twelve days of school, for snow or for resulting flooding. As it was not possible to make up all the school days we had missed, we teachers were told to put the pressure on for the remainder of the year and to work the students as hard as we could, stressing the basic skills.

One afternoon, after a particularly trying day, the principal looked up at me from where he was sitting in the office, shook his head, sighed, and said, "Next year, don't study the weather. Study something safe, like maybe rattlesnakes!"

Prayer:

Our Heavenly Father, Teach us to appreciate and respect the forces of nature. Amen.

Shortcuts

> He becometh poor that dealeth with a slack hand: but the hand of the diligent maketh rich.
>
> Proverbs 10:4

I was assigned to teach a class on basic living skills to the fifth and sixth grade students. One of the skills that we attacked was sewing. I provided the students with needle and thread, and we learned to thread the needle, tie a knot, and do a simple running stitch. We applied these skills to the art of making a pillow. The students cut an animal shape out of two pieces of fabric. They pinned the shapes, right sides together, and sewed a quarter-inch seam around the edges of the animal, leaving one small opening for turning the pillow right side out and stuffing.

I told my students that they should have six to eight running stitches per inch. Most of the students had a ruler readily available to measure their rate of stitching.

Nevertheless some of the children took shortcuts. They were in such a hurry to see the finished product that they rushed and took huge stitches (about an inch long each!). Whenever I saw this, I took out my sharp scissors and ripped out their work.

"Ohhh…," they would groan.

"You must start again," I would say.

Occasionally a student would get by me. He would lay low as I made my rounds, and I wouldn't catch him with his too-big stitches.

But his evasion would be short-lived. When he would turn his pillow right side out and stuff it, the stuffing would start to ooze out of the holes. Eventually some of the stitches would come out, and the student's reward for his hastiness would be a sloppy, unattractive pillow.

Prayer:

Dear God, Grant us the patience to do all our tasks on this earth to the best of our abilities so we won't have to undo or redo them at a later time, and so that we are pleased with the results. Amen.

Yes, Toni?

> Therefore I will look unto the Lord; I will wait for the God of my salvation: my God will hear me.
>
> Micah 7:7

Fifth graders love to tell stories. When our science lesson touched on a topic that the children had some experience with, their little hands would be reaching for the sky, their little eyes wide open, eager, and pleading for me to call on them.

One of my little girls, Toni, had a story for every topic. She was quite a talker, Toni was, and her stories would sometimes last five minutes or more.

"Yes, Toni?" I would say. And the story would start. I would shift my weight from one leg to the other. Eventually I would pull up my stool and sit down. Toni's story would be animated with facial expressions and hand/arm gestures. The class would listen patiently. Occasionally I would see eyes look to the ceiling and a head or two shake in disbelief. I would hear an occasional sigh and a stifled yawn.

I believe the class tolerated Toni's stories, perhaps because the students thought that the more they listened, the less work they would have to do in class. (Or maybe Mrs. Moore would forget about assigning homework.)

Toni's stories would bring up story ideas to most of the children, and my class would become a sea of hands waving to be called on next. I always knew at this point that I had lost control. And if the topic had anything to do with animals or animal behavior, you might as well put the books and papers away and pull up the stool permanently.

How can you not give every child the opportunity to talk about a subject so near and dear to them as their pets?

How can I channel this interest and energy into the study of science? I wondered one evening. The science fair was coming up in a few months. Perhaps…

The next morning, I asked, "How could you use a pet of yours to conduct a scientific investigation?"

"Are you suggesting I dissect my dog?" asked James.

"No, but is there a question you could ask and then manipulate materials and see how your pet reacts?" I asked.

The class started to stir. Here was the topic of pets again. A few hands went up, including Toni's. I overlooked hers, for now. I sensed she had a story, and this wasn't a good time.

"Which lure do the fish prefer?" suggested Stan, pointing to our aquarium of native West Virginia fish.

"Describe some of the lures you would try," I said.

The students mentioned rubber worms, salamanders, spinners…

"Do rubber worms come in a variety of colors?" I asked.

"Sure," said Stan.

"How about a variety of sizes?" I said.

"Yes, or you can take a big one and cut it into whatever size you want," said Bill.

"Very good. Now you're thinking," I said.

Toni's hand went up. Her eyes were wide open, a story ready to pour out. I ignored her.

"Stan," I continued, "Can you state the question, and this time, limit the experiment to only one variable?"

"How about, 'Does the size of a lure affect the minnows' reaction to it?'" asked Stan.

"What things would you keep constant?" I asked.

"The color of the lure, the speed and the depth it is put into the water, the time of day you do the experiment…" said Stan.

"Excellent," I said.

Toni's hand was still waving, but I didn't want anything to break the continuity of the lesson at this point.

We spent the majority of the class period coming up with ideas for science fair projects. The students were exceptionally motivated.

"Does the age of a cat affect its ability to learn tricks?" said Brenda.

"Very good," I said.

"What dog food does my dog prefer?" said Shawn.

Toni's hand shot up. I ignored it.

"These sound like very interesting investigations," I said. "For homework, I want you all to think of a question you would like to answer using the scientific method. It can deal with any topic, not just pets," I said.

I looked at my watch. I looked at Toni's waving hand. About five minutes of class time remained. I thought we had had a productive science lesson, and the children were inspired to start planning their science fair projects at home. Now, what do we do to fill the last five minutes of class? I reached for my stool.

"Yes, Toni?" I said.

Prayer:

Dear Lord, Let there be time and patience to hear all the children's voices. Amen.

Labels

> Beloved, let us love one another: for love is of God; and every one that loveth is born of God, and knoweth God.
>
> 1 John 4:7

Children are so ready to label each other—this one's a dweeb; this one's a nerd; this one's cool; this one's dumb, etc. I never was quite sure what a dweeb was or how it was distinguished from a nerd, but I knew how a child's face would fall when he became labeled as one of the uncomplimentary types. The labels would often stick with a child for years and trouble them for years to come.

When Tippy outgrew his puppy collar, Alison and I went shopping for a new one. She chose one of leather so that her daddy could punch extra holes in it to make it fit the dog's neck just right. And she picked a red one, as she thought that red was indeed Tippy's color.

One day Tippy got caught in a rainstorm. We brought him home, and while Dan fluffed Tippy's fur with a towel and I went for the hair dryer, Alison took off his collar.

"Oooh, look!" she wailed. "Look at Tippy's neck! It's red!"

We gathered around to see that the new leather collar had bled red dye all around the white fur of Tippy's neck.

"Tippy is a redneck! Tippy is a redneck!" Dan chanted.

"Don't call my doggy names," I said.

Dan continued to tease Tippy about being a redneck until Alison realized that a redneck referred to a type of person.

"Daddy, what is a redneck?" Alison asked.

"Well," he said, and proceeded to give Alison his definition of what a redneck is. Suffice it to say that Alison was not pleased with his definition.

When Dan finished, Alison looked up at him.

"Daddy, can we go back to the store?" she asked.

"Why, honey?" Dan said.

"I want to get Tippy a new collar—a blue one this time."

Prayer:

Dear Lord, Let us avoid the labels that hurt and separate us from others. Amen.

> # Hey!

And the *Lord* came, and stood, and called as at other times, *Samuel, Samuel.* Then Samuel answered, Speak; for thy servant heareth.
> 1 Samuel 3:10

One afternoon my students were particularly noisy, and I yelled, "Hey!" to get their attention and to quiet them down. Immediately, Freddie got out of his seat and came up to me.

"Did you call me, Mrs. Moore?" he asked.
"No, Freddie. I said 'Hey!,'" I told him.

"Oh," Freddie said, as he shrugged his shoulders and turned to walk back to his seat. "Well, that's what they call me at home!"

Prayer:
Our Father, When You call our name, let us hear.

Basic Needs

But my God shall supply all your need according to his riches in glory by Christ Jesus.

> Philippians 4:19

The Kanawha Charleston Humane Association has the rule that any dog or cat that you adopt from them needs to be neutered or spayed. The animals are to have no food or water after eight o'clock the evening before their surgery.

I fixed Tippy his favorite mix of dry and canned dog food at seven thirty and watched him gobble it down. He then took a long drink from a bowl of cool water I had set out for him. I was concerned that he would become thirsty during the night, so I led him to his water bowl several more times before the eight o'clock deadline. Then, promptly at eight, I poured the remaining water down the drain, washed out his food dish, and put the two bowls away to reduce any temptation for the dog.

About nine thirty, Tippy walked over to his feeding area and stood. He then tipped back to the living room and plopped down on the rug with a sigh.

At ten o'clock, I gave Tippy a pat and said, "Good night, boy. See you in the morning."

Around two in the morning, I was awakened by the sound of Tippy knocking a plastic bottle over and pushing it across the floor. I stumbled into the hallway to find Tippy chewing on a bottle of bleach. Tippy was not in the habit of chewing anything but his toys, and he appeared to be interested in the bleach bottle because of the liquid he heard sloshing around in it.

"No, boy, no!" I said as I rescued the bleach bottle. Tippy walked over to his feeding area and stood looking at me. "I'm sorry, Tip, I can't give you anything," I whined.

I led him back to the living room rug. He lay down and I turned off the lights.

At about two forty-five, I was awakened again—this time by a loud *thump* in the bathroom. I crawled out of bed and flipped on the bathroom light to find Tippy in the bathtub, licking a bath sponge.

"Tippy, come!" I said. I called to my husband to help me get the dog out of the tub. Tippy immediately went to his feeding area and stood. When he saw that I wasn't going to give him anything, he began pacing from the bathroom, to his feeding area, back to the bathroom, to his feeding area.

I was close to tears.

"I can't leave him like this," I said. "He's getting desperate for water. He'll be up all night."

I watched Tippy pace back and forth. He paid no attention to us in his search for water.

I finally broke down and poured a trickle of water into his water bowl. It was barely enough to wet his tongue, and he lapped it up greedily. When the water was gone, he returned to the living room and plopped down with a sigh.

Tippy made it through the night, but I spent about thirty sleepless minutes. In our land of plenty, I had never before seen a living thing suffer from lack of his basic needs. How agonizing it had been to watch the dog desperately search for water when the pipelines of the house were full of it. I thought of the children in our country who go to bed hungry. Can they live with the fact that tons of food from restaurants and schools are daily thrown away? Can they understand a world where some bakeries throw away day-old donuts?

My thoughts traveled to the Third World countries, where the need for food, clothing, and shelter is even more pronounced. Do children from these countries know of our high standards of living? Do they go to bed at night thinking life is unfair?

Prayer:

Our Heavenly Father, Let us share the riches of life with those less fortunate than ourselves. Let our money and gifts find appropriate channels through which they will do the most good. Amen.

Quiet Little Girls

A good man out of the good treasure of his heart bringeth forth that which is good;

Luke 6:45

A growing concern among educators is the fact that at some point, usually in the middle grades, many little girls tend to close up. They stop raising their hands, and they stop volunteering for activities. These quiet little girls are often passive and unassertive.

Although this tendency of young girls worries me, I have found that often my best writers are these quiet little girls who open up with pen and paper in a way one would never expect from their introverted outward appearance. They have found a vent through the written word, an avenue of communication with which they are comfortable. Although they may not be noticed as readily, their words may stick around for a while.

Write on, little girls!

Prayer:

Dear Lord, Help even the quiet people store up and pour out good things. Amen.

Rewards

> For his anger endureth but a moment; in his favor is life: weeping may endure for a night, but joy cometh in the morning.
>
> Psalm 30:5

"For my science fair project, can I see what kind of dog food Tippy prefers?" asked my daughter, Alison.

"Well, that project has been done quite a few times by other students. Can you think of something else?" I asked.

"I want to use Tippy in my experiment," she said.

"Scientists have come a long way in their research in animal behavior," I said. "Quite a few facts that I learned in school have since been proven to be untrue. Get some books on dogs, and see if there are any facts you would like to test out."

Alison came home from school the next day with a book about dogs.

"There's a whole section on how a dog sees things," she said. "Are they really color-blind?" she asked.

"That's what I've always heard," I said.

"Tippy is smart. I think he could pick out one color from another," she declared.

"That sounds like an interesting project," I said. "How would you do it?"

Alison decided that she would teach Tippy "red" with a piece of construction paper.

"Red, red, red," she said, holding up the red paper as Tippy sat and watched. "Red, red, red," she repeated over and over.

"Where's red?" she asked and, to our surprise, Tippy touched the red paper with his nose.

"Good boy!" we said.

Alison went through the same procedure with a blue piece of construction paper.

"Blue, blue, blue," she said. "Blue, blue, blue. Where's blue?"

Tippy touched the blue paper with his nose. We were ecstatic.

Next Alison held up the red paper and the blue paper side by side.

"Where's red?" she asked.

Tippy touched the red paper with his front paw.

"Good boy!" Alison said.

When she asked for blue, he found it. When she asked for red, again he found it. Alison altered the side at which she held each color to ensure that the dog was indeed choosing on the basis of color and not just on the position of the paper.

For the next evening or two, Tippy chose the appropriate color with 100 percent accuracy and was rewarded with praise and a pat on the head. Then, he seemed to lose interest in the game. He would actually walk away from Alison when she got the papers out.

"Maybe we need to try a different reward," I said. "Let's get some bologna."

I took a piece of bologna and cut it into eight small pieces. I showed Tippy the bologna, then I stood behind Alison. She held out the two pieces of paper in front of Tippy's now attentive face.

"Where's red?" she asked. Tippy reached up with his front paw and touched the red paper.

"Good boy!" we said, as I placed the bologna within his reach. He snapped it up.

"Tippy, where's blue?" said Alison. He pawed at the blue paper, gobbled his reward, and stood at attention.

Alison decided to introduce two new colors to Tippy. She chose pink and light orange because she felt they were closer in color than the red and blue were.

"Pink, pink, pink. Where's pink?"

Tippy pawed the pink. He got his bologna.

"Orange, orange, orange. Where's orange?"

Tippy pawed the orange. He got his bologna.

Each time Alison held up both the pink and the orange paper, Tippy responded correctly and was rewarded with his favorite treat, bologna. In fact, Tippy cooperated so enthusiastically that several times, as he pawed at the paper, he actually shredded it with his toenails. Tippy responded correctly 100 percent of the time when any combination of the four different colors were used. We were impressed with our little dog's ability and amused at what he could accomplish, all for a little piece of bologna.

Prayer:
Our Heavenly Father, Guide us as we work toward our reward with you in heaven. Amen.

The Artist

For the body is not one member, but many.
1 Corinthians 12:14

Nelson was constantly drawing. If I lectured, he drew. If I assigned a page of bookwork, he would finish it rapidly, and then draw. If I showed a movie, he drew. About the only time he would give up drawing was when we were doing a hands-on activity in science class, and his hands would be too busy to draw. But his paper and pencil were never very far away.

I was worried that Nelson wasn't paying adequate attention to his class work, yet he scored well on tests, made high grades, and received an academic letter at the awards banquet. Obviously, Nelson's drawing in class was not hindering his achievement. He was not obvious about his artwork, so none of the other students complained. I could have insisted that he put the drawing away, for the principle of the thing, but I didn't want to taint our good teacher/student relationship or perhaps crush his creativity and drive. I could see the headlines now: "Artistic genius Nelson Smith claims his fifth grade teacher forbid him to draw!"

Never!

So I let Nelson draw. He seemed to be a happy productive little fellow, and I was satisfied with his achievement.

Research is showing that there is a variety of different learning styles and that some people learn better under different environmental conditions. Maybe Nelson needs to doodle, just as some people learn better with a noisy background, while others, like myself, need silence. My parents thought they were doing right by buying me a fine wooden desk, a straight back chair, and a bright desk lamp for me to use as a child as I did my homework, and how I must have frustrated them when they would see me lounging on the bed doing my homework in diffuse light.

These factors, plus the fact that some students learn best when they see information in writing, some learn best when they hear a lesson orally, and some learn best when they are actively involved in a hands-on approach, truly challenge a teacher to present lessons in a manner that will catch each student in the way that he learns best.

Prayer:
Dear Lord, Help us to reach each child. Amen.

Abandoned

Blessed are ye that hunger now: for ye shall be filled. Blessed are ye that weep now: for ye shall laugh.

Luke 6:21

Alison and I were en route to the school one evening in May to attend the yearly Academic Awards Banquet. As I drove down the exit ramp of the interstate, there, in a nearby field, was a copper-colored dog, standing, watching traffic.

"Look, Mommy! Can we get him?" Alison asked.

I explained to her how it was dangerous to deal with adult dogs when you don't know their background.

"Anyway, he's probably somebody's dog just out for a run," I said. We drove on.

Several hours later as we approached the interstate, the last portion of our journey home, I glanced over at the exit ramp. There sat the copper-colored dog, just at the edge of the road where his owners had probably abandoned him. He had followed his tracks from the field where we had first seen him back to where they had probably begun—by the road. He sat patiently, aware that the daylight hours were coming to a close but trusting that he would be cared for.

The next morning I watched for the copper-colored dog on my way to school, but he was nowhere to be seen. Did his owners come back for him? I doubt it. Had a loving caring person who will see to his needs picked him up? Slim chance. Did he wander off and try to survive by raiding garbage cans or begging door to door? That's a possibility. Did he meet up with a pack of dogs who were also abandoned at one time by their owners and who now cause destruction to wildlife and livestock? Very possibly. Or had a car struck him down as he wandered around in the vicinity of the interstate last night? A distinct possibility. God only knows.

Prayer:

Our Heavenly Father, Help us to see the necessity of limiting pet populations and caring for existing dependent animals. Amen.

> "The"

> Now the God of patience and consolation grant you to be likeminded one toward another according to Christ Jesus.
>
> Romans 15:5

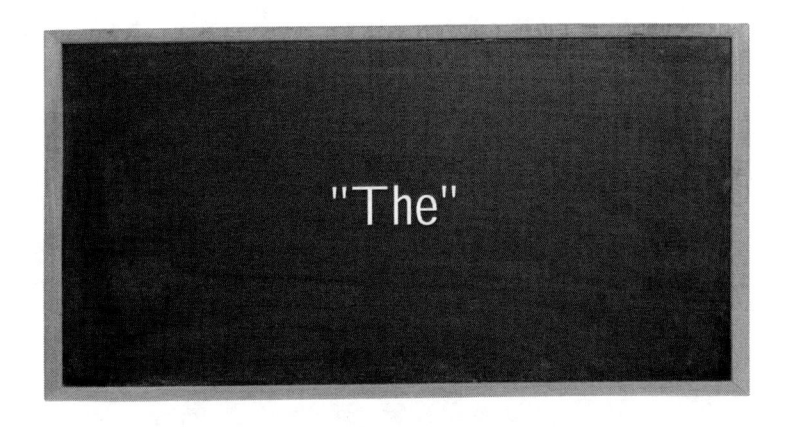

Occasionally, when no teacher was available to cover in-school suspension, a seventh or eighth grader had to spend the day in my fifth grade class. One morning I was told that Mark, an eighth grader, was going to spend the day with us. He was to sit in a seat away from the fifth graders, was to do all the fifth grade work, was to eat lunch with the younger students, take breaks and recess with us, etc.

Mark had been a student of mine last school year. We had had a good relationship, and I wanted to make sure that nothing happened to spoil that. I explained to my class that Mark was going to spend the day with us and why and that they were to avoid making eye contact with him or attracting his attention in any way.

When Mark walked into our classroom, I directed him to a seat in the back of the room, and we began our science lesson. He kept his head down, obviously embarrassed at his predicament. The morning went well, with no flare-ups, although I could hardly keep from giggling when I lined my class up for lunch and saw Mark towering over my other students.

After lunch, I assigned an activity to all students based of the eight parts of speech. My fifth graders dove into it. We had worked on nouns, verbs, pronouns, adjectives, adverbs, conjunctions, prepositions, and interjections all year, and the students knew them well. As a review, I assigned four sentences from a book we had read, and the students were to classify each word according to its part of speech. I told them they could use their English books, but nobody did. They were confident.

Mark looked over at me from the corner of his eye. He wagged his finger at me; I approached him.

"Are you going to turn this in to my English teacher for a grade?" he whispered.

"Probably will," I whispered back.

Mark groaned and pulled out his book.

I circled the classroom slowly. My fifth graders were buzzing away with the assignment. As I turned to begin my rounds again, I noticed Mark's hand in the air.

"Mrs. Moore, what is *the*?" he whined.

I had just drilled the fifth graders the day before on the articles *a*, *an*, and *the*. They knew these to be adjectives. Now, the fifth graders had been told to ignore Mark and pretend that he wasn't there, but they couldn't help themselves. They didn't look at Mark, but they looked at each other and giggled. Imagine, this big, tough eighth grader not knowing what *the* was. Unthinkable!

"Use your book," I said.

My students dutifully kept their heads down over their work, but their eyes occasionally shifted over to Mark. They eyed his obvious confusion and frustration with the assignment and then looked at me to see my reaction. I covered my smile, but my eyes gave my amusement away.

Mark eventually detected and joined in on our quiet merriment. By the end of the day, he was talking out to my students and winking at my little girls, who thought that was the weirdest behavior ever!

We all went home that day with smiles on our faces. The fifth graders were tickled that they could do an assignment that an eighth grader had problems with. Mark had had a day without getting into trouble, although he hopefully realized he had some catching up to do in grammar. And I, with the overwhelming support of my little fifth graders, had thoroughly enjoyed a day which had had the potential of being a difficult one.

Prayer:

Dear Lord, Help us to work together to make every day a good one. Amen.

Drivin' It Home

> Thou madest him to have dominion over the works of thy hands: thou hast put all things under his feet:
>
> Psalms 8:6

I had promised the worker at the Kanawha Charleston Humane Association that our forty-eight fifth graders would be very well behaved when we came to visit the animal shelter. My colleague and I had prepared the students for the trip by explaining what kinds of behaviors we expected and what kinds of behaviors we would not tolerate.

The students cooperated with exemplary behavior at the other stops on the field trip: the Charleston Cultural Center, the National Weather Station, and at the Wendy's restaurant. The waitress even asked the children what school they were from and complimented them on their behavior.

We walked up the steps to the animal shelter, the last stop on the field trip, and I announced our arrival to the worker who was going to take us on a tour of the shelter. As the students squeezed into the tiny waiting room, they caught their first glimpse of animals—kittens in the display window.

"Oooh, how cute!"

"Look at that one!"

"Let me see…"

"I like the black one!"

The orderly group of young ladies and gentlemen had turned into a lively mass of excited children. I quieted them down enough to introduce the worker. She was a petite lady who could barely be seen above the students who were standing directly in front of her. She unfortunately could not compete with the kittens.

As we approached the puppy room, the dogs in the dog runs must have sensed our enormous presence and compounded the worker's difficulties by barking strenuously. I could see her at the head of the line; her mouth was moving, but her words did not reach my ears.

At that point, the worker decided to just lead us through the rest of the shelter and let the students see all the animals. That was fine. I had already prepared the students for this visit. I had shared the statistics that showed what a large number of cats and dogs had to be destroyed each year as the quantity of animals dropped off at the shelter or picked up as strays greatly outnumbered the total adoptions. I had explained the behaviors necessary to be a responsible pet owner and to prevent unwanted litters. I know that these were the messages that the worker would have told us if we hadn't overwhelmed her.

The dogs, with their pleading eyes and wagging tails, would drive the message home.

Prayer:

Dear Lord, Bless the animals of the world, who serve us as companions, diversions, inspirations, and delights. Amen.

Grand Old Stories

> The grass withereth, the flower fadeth: but
> the word of our God shall stand for ever.
> Isaiah 40:8

Alison will be a fifth grader this coming school year. She let me know that I was "getting old" when I started telling her a "When I was a little girl" story, and she said, "Oh, no, not again!"

I remember not being very appreciative of my mother's girlhood stories that she tried to tell me when I was young. But how precious those stories are to me now.

Mom spent some of her preschool years living in Detroit, Michigan. This was between the years 1924 and 1928. She tells of a time when a woman with an infant in a baby buggy interrupted my mom while she was playing on the sidewalk and asked her, at age four, to watch over the infant while the woman went into a store. How the world has changed since then!

One of Mom's favorite stories is about the time her new half-slip fell off while she was walking home from school. She must have been around seven or eight years old, when little girls still don't have a well-defined waist to hold such things as a skirt or half-slip up. She was so embarrassed that she ran the short distance home and absolutely refused to go back and retrieve the slip, which lay on the sidewalk and whose story, as far as my mother was concerned, ended there.

Today's inflation would not allow my great-grandmother to be so creative in saying "no!" as she was in the 1930s. When my mother would ask to go to a movie in town, her grandmother would tell her to "Go watch for a dime rolling up the street." What we need for a movie today won't even roll!

Another favorite story involves my mom and her sister and the penny candy store. The girls had been instructed to only buy candy that had a wrapper on it. Their mother was concerned that anything unwrapped may have been touched by unclean hands. On one outing to the candy store, my mom was attracted to a particularly tempting new kind of candy that, unfortunately, was not enclosed in a wrapper. Mom solved that problem by purchasing the candy and, on her way home, picking up a piece of paper on the street and wrapping her candy in it.

The last time we visited my mom, I caught her and Alison laughing together.

"You told her the slip story, didn't you?" I asked.

Mom nodded, wiping away the happy tears.

I'm sorry I wasn't a better listener when I was younger, Mom. Maybe Alison can make it up to you, for me.

Prayer:

Dear God, Thank you for grandmothers who have the time to tell sweet stories to little listening ears. Amen.

Balls of Fur

*Are not two sparrows sold for a farthing?
And one of them shall not fall on the ground
without your Father.*

Matthew 10:29

My class's visit to the pound in the spring may have led to several adoptions. I know it resulted in one for certain.

Alison and I visit the pound often to drop off newspapers or little crafted items that the workers sell for dollar donations to the animal shelter, and on each visit, we always check out the animals.

When I stopped by to schedule a time for my class to visit, Alison and I strolled the length of the dog runs, visiting with the shelter's canine occupants.

A little white and black fur ball came trotting to the door of her pen. As we talked to her, she whined, pressed her body into the corner nearest us, turned her nose skyward, and twisted her head provocatively, with one eye focused on us. As she batted the eye, I noticed that she had eyelashes, one white and the other black. How feminine and sweet she looked compared to rugged old Tippy!

I said to Alison, "Look, she wants to come to us," but then she immediately got to her feet and trotted outside to greet a family who was checking out the exterior pens.

"She's strange looking," said Alison. "What kind is she?"

Alison had me there. We went to the library, found several books on dogs, and began to narrow the choices down.

"She looks like an Akita," I said. "Except I don't see any with markings like hers. I don't know where she got those unusual spots."

The next day we again went to the animal shelter, supposedly to confirm my class's scheduled visit but, subconsciously, I think I had an ulterior motive. And this time I brought my husband.

"Look at her," I said, stopping in front of the fur ball's cage. She was stretched out on the floor asleep. The black eye-lashed side of her face was up, revealing splotches and swirls of black on a white background, topped with a black pointed ear that stood up like a cat's. As we talked in front of her cage, her head raised to show the pure white side, also topped with a black ear.

"Where did you get that face?" Dan asked her. The fluffy tail wagged vigorously.

Alison and I worked on Dan for about twenty-four hours. He eventually got tired of our hounding and returned to the pound and signed the adoption papers. Little Panda became our second dog and Tippy's beloved playmate.

Dan gave me strict instructions that I may stop by the waiting room at the animal shelter, but under no circumstances am I to visit the dog runs again. (Do you really think I obey?) I think his resistance is even lower than mine, but at least he has the sense to stay away. To me, it's sad that the people who care the most about the homeless animals are the ones who must stay away because they lack the resources to save all the little (and big) balls of fur. And sometimes the tug on one's heart is just a little too hard.

Prayer:

Dear God, Bless the people who care for our homeless animals, a necessary but sometimes heart-wrenching job. Amen.

Rules

> And let the peace of God rule in your hearts, to the which also ye are called in one body; and be ye thankful.
>
> Colossians 3:15

We teachers encourage our students every year to take the standardized tests very seriously. The test results are used to judge the students' abilities and the school's effectiveness. I remember taking a test as a high school student and being distracted by another student continuously tapping a pencil on his desk, so I warn my students against doing anything that might distract another test-taker. The students are allowed to chew gum, but may not crack or pop it. The students are not to talk to each other for any reason during a test.

I noticed, during the first section of the test, that a few of the fifth graders finished the test early and were communicating with each other through gestures and lip reading. This behavior was distracting some of the students who were not yet finished with their testing.

"All right," I said, after the students finished the first test. "I don't want you communicating in any way, shape, or form! When you finish a test, get your silent reading out or a piece of paper to draw on, but don't make eye contact with each other! When you're looking at each other, the next thing I know you're communicating with each other, and we can't have that. No eye contact!"

Having warned the students of dire consequences if they ignored the rules, I got them started taking the second part of the test. This section tested the students' reading comprehension and involved the students reading a page of writing and then answering questions about what they had read. This test was sixty minutes long and required long intervals of intense concentration on the part of the students. I quietly made the rounds of my classroom, monitoring the students' progress.

"*AhChhhooo…!*"

I think we all rose about five inches off our seats at that point. I looked over in the direction from which the sound had come, and there was Chad, looking at me with alarm in his eyes. I guess this little guy was afraid that a sneeze was a punishable offense. Our eyes locked for a second or two and, before I could assure Chad that everything was cool, his mouth suddenly shot open; his eyebrows popped up; the alarm in his eyes increased threefold; his chin then plummeted on his chest, and his eyes dropped to his test.

Eye contact! Chad realized that after his explosive sneeze, he had made eye contact with, no less, his teacher!

I slipped through the doorway for a minute to hide my merriment. Poor little guy. Chad was a sensitive little boy, and I guess maybe my rules were a bit overwhelming to him. Thank you, Chad, for taking your teacher so seriously, and we'll laugh about it later, after the test, of course.

Prayer:

Our Heavenly Father, Let us look to you for the rules of life. Amen.

Symbols

Wherefore by their fruits they shall be known.
Matthew 8:20

Some elementary school teachers live by the philosophy that every day they should wear something distinctive that the students will notice, like a pin or a badge or a necklace. I came to the middle school as one of a few elementary teachers amidst a crew of secondary school teachers, and I soon came to be known as "Necklace Woman."

Actually, I only had about four necklaces that I wore regularly, but they were big, bold, and noticeable. I had a large wooden heart suspended from a scarf, a sizable wooden apple of similar design, a ribbon of wooden watermelon slices, and a string of red, white, and blue wooden disks. But my collection readily grew as a couple of secret pals and a particular librarian took it upon themselves to shower me with pendants.

The librarian, Laura Bell, was especially generous, and all of her necklaces symbolized something. One day after I had picked up some craft supplies in Charleston for her, I found a note and a necklace in my mailbox. Another time, after I had helped her sort through some library books, I found a necklace hanging from a hook in my classroom. But the year Laura Bell became my not-so-secret pal was the year my necklace collection got out of control. I received necklaces in autumn colors, Christmas tree and snowman necklaces, Valentine hearts on strings, patriotic necklaces with stars and stripes, teacher necklaces with miniature chalkboards and apples, and Easter bunny and egg necklaces.

Shortly before Laura Bell retired last year, I heard her mention her dogs.

"What dogs?" I asked.

"I have a couple of pound doggies, too," she said. "I guess my resistance is pretty low, just like yours."

I miss Laura Bell. I miss her sympathetic ear and her periodic visits to my classroom. Laura Bell was one who would never turn a child away and was always ready with assuring words, a hug, or a Kleenex whenever the need arose. After thirty years of teaching at the same school, Laura Bell's retirement left a void that will be difficult to fill.

Which necklace shall I wear today? As I finger through the myriad of necklaces which are hanging from a hook in my bathroom, as no jewelry box or drawer is large enough for my enormous collection, I choose my favorite, a large black Scotty dog suspended on a navy bandana. I must be careful as I bend down to help the students today. My Scotty dog is so large it may swing from its support and knock someone on the head.

Thank you, Laura Bell, for giving me little things that may help me attract my students' attention. They may truly listen when I "bark" today. And thank you for all the remembrances and symbols of our friendship and our years of working together.

Prayer:

Dear Lord, Let us through our acts and deeds act as symbols of the Christian way of life. Amen.

Fidos and Fifth Graders

O Lord, how manifold are thy works! in wisdom hast thou made them all: the earth is full of thy riches.

Psalms 104:24

I delight in recognizing the similarities in the behavior of children and canines...

Our Tippy reacts differently to different people, different stimuli, and different situations. When he's playful, he seeks out Alison, who has endless energy and who romps unselfishly with him. When

Tippy wants a change in environment, he finds my husband, who is apt to take him for a walk or a run in the woods. But when the dog is hungry or tired, he comes to me. I am the dispenser of food. I am the one at whose feet he can lie quietly while I type at the word processor.

Tippy is normally well behaved in the house, but give him a bath, and he runs pell-mell from one end of the trailer to the other, ending with a flying leap on the mauve couch. I remember when about twenty inches of snow knocked out electric lines and subzero temperatures forced us to take daughter, dog, and parakeets to a nearby motel. The "good boy" entertained himself by jumping back and forth from one king-sized bed to the other repeatedly.

Children will also surprise you when situations are changed. Some of the most ornery young ones will be virtual angels on a field trip. Yet when parents visit the classroom, some children choose this time to show off and misbehave.

Currently, the trend in science and mathematics education emphasizes the importance of hands-on experiences for children. Before you try to teach the students anything with mirrors, counters, or rocks and seeds, it is recommended that the students be allowed to handle the materials, investigate and experiment with them, even play with them before the children are expected to work with the materials. Once the students get the urge to fiddle with the materials out of their systems, they usually are more settled and work better throughout the activity.

I see similar needs in my dog. We have decided that Tippy is a coonhound mix, which helps to explain his high energy level and his love of running through the hills and meadows of West Virginia. I have frustrated myself trying to teach Tippy to walk at my side on his leash before he has had an opportunity to get his daily run, because the lesson ends up an episode of Tippy dragging me for a walk, which satisfies neither him nor me. Yet, when Tippy returns from his daily run, I let him lap up a drink of water, and he is content to heel along with me to my heart's content.

It tickles me to take my dogs for a ride in the car. My husband and daughter take the back seat, as Tippy and Panda sit in the front seat with their noses pressed against one of the vents, sniffing at the world as we go by. In Dan's vent-less truck, the dogs usually lie down for a nap, but in my car they attentively "see the sights" through their nostrils. I wonder what all they can detect with their olfactory glands. They obviously prefer their sense of smell to their sense of sight, as their eyes are focused on the vents also. I keep threatening to allow my husband to drive my car as the dogs and I put our noses to the vent. No doubt I would soon peek over the top of the dash to see what I was missing.

Could we learn another lesson from the dogs? Tippy was our only dog for over a year. He got the undivided attention of my husband, my daughter, and myself. Then came Panda.

Getting a second dog in the family was wonderful for Tippy. Panda was a companion to frolic with, someone to run at his heels through the hills, but we soon learned that we had to be careful. If we petted Panda first, Tippy would become very still, as an angry glare stole over his eyes. If we continued to make a fuss over Panda, she would usually suffer a nip from the older dog.

We learned that Tippy must receive his treat a second or two before Panda does. That way he is occupied with eating while we are handing the younger dog her treat. We learned that we must pat Tippy first and last, or he will put little Panda in her place. My daughter loves to call out the dogs' names as she plays with them. She learned, at Panda's expense, that she shouldn't say Panda's name more than she does Tippy's as it appears that Tippy was keeping score and perhaps counting the number of times each name was said. (I guess talking and distinguishing colors was not enough for Tippy, and he felt the need to get into mathematics!)

Little Panda is quite content to be the underdog. Her little eyes are bright and happy no matter if Tippy is the first to be fed or patted. She is fully content to run a few steps behind Tippy and to wait until he is finished eating before she starts. She knows he is alpha and that she must wait. And now that my family and I understand some of the complexities of the dog hierarchy, we can adjust our behavior so that everyone is happy.

Many of my friends say that a major problem in their families is sibling rivalry; brothers and sisters quarrelling amongst themselves for whatever reasons. I think of how often I have made a fuss over someone's newborn baby and perhaps comparatively overlooked his or her older children.

Maybe there is a lesson to be learned from the dogs…

Prayer:

Dear Lord, Help us to recognize the complexities of animal and human behavior that we may live in peace and harmony. Amen.

Bombs Away!

> But thou, O man of God, flee these things; and follow after righteousness, godliness, faith, love, patience, meekness.
>
> 1 Timothy 6:11

Fifth grade seems to be a time when some of the little boys are so clumsy. Their bodies are growing at rapid and irregular rates; they are becoming self-conscious about their physical appearance, and the end result is that they frequently tend to trip over, run into, and knock over anything that gets in the way.

Charlie sat beside me and across from Mr. Hicks the other fifth grade teacher, at the Wendy's restaurant during our stop for lunch on our field trip. As Mr. Hicks and I chatted about how the day was progressing; Charlie was opening ketchup packets for his French fries. Before long, I felt a warm, wet sensation on my left arm. I looked down to see a blob of ketchup oozing toward my elbow. My eyes traveled over to Charlie, who was staring at me, his teeth clenched nervously and his mouth widened into a grin. As he blinked sheepishly, I saw the opened and overturned ketchup packet that he had been squeezing over his French fries.

"Oops," he said, as he pasted the smile back on his face.

"Good shot," I said, eying Charlie over my glasses as I wiped away the ketchup.

I continued talking with Mr. Hicks, and then I turned to converse with students sitting on the other side of me. Our conversation was interrupted by the crash and tinkle of glass breaking. The noise sounded as if the accident happened close by, but I had seen nothing fall and could not tell from which direction the sound came. As I pivoted in my seat, my eyes eventually took in Charlie's face. He was looking sheepishly at me, with his teeth clenched and his smile a little less in diameter, more like a grimace. I surveyed the top of Charlie's table and, seeing nothing out of the ordinary, I bent down to look under the table. There on the floor lay a glass ashtray, shattered.

I looked at Charlie. "How did you manage that?" I asked.

"Ahh, I moved over to make room for Ricky," he said, "and the table sort of tipped." He bent down to pick up the pieces of broken glass.

"No!" I said. "You'll get cut. Go tell one of the waitresses what happened."

I scooted my chair out of the way while the waitress bent down to pick up the glass.

"Ow!" she cried, as she picked a shard of glass out of her finger and a small line of blood surfaced. She wrapped her finger in a napkin while I helped her pick up the remaining pieces of glass.

While the waitress went to get a sweeper, I said to Charlie, "Why don't you sit over there so you can finish your lunch."

"Ahh, Nancy," said Mr. Hicks. "Are you sure you want him sitting there?"

I turned around to see a row of empty tables and, beyond it, the lunch crowd from the Capitol and the steady flow of traffic on Washington Street.

"I see no problem," I said, shrugging my shoulders.

"Plate glass," Mr. Hicks whispered. "The window?"

"Oh, wait, Charlie. Take my place. Here, I'm finished."

I hopped out of my seat. I steered Charlie into my chair, and I moved into the seat across from him.

The rest of our noontime meal was relatively uneventful. But when Charlie later went through the food line again and came back with a fresh supply of French fries and ketchup, I figured it was time for me to empty my tray, so I excused myself before Charlie's ketchup could make a frontal attack.

Prayer:

Our Heavenly Father, Please grant us the patience necessary to deal with these changing young people. Help us to understand them as they are trying to understand themselves. Amen.

Paw Prints on My Back

> As far as the east is from the west, so far hath
> he removed our transgressions from us.
> Psalms 103:12

Panda was taught at an early age to greet us with all four paws on the ground. Although I enjoy a good romp with my dogs, past experiences with Tippy and some of my friends have taught me that not everybody appreciates such occurrences.

As my husband was digging for the footers and the pipelines for our house, Panda would amuse herself by splashing in the pools of water that collected in the trenches, the white dog emerging and dripping with the red clay mud. This was further incentive for us to encourage her not to jump up on us.

But Panda would catch me when my back was turned, literally. If I would kneel down to examine a flower or study a stone, "*Splaat*!" Panda would slap her front paws on my back, leaving muddy prints.

One day, after a few hours of playing with the dogs, Alison and I stopped at the grocery store for a few items.

"Mom," Alison whispered. "You've got paw prints on your back."

The paw prints on my back told the world that Panda had been a "bad girl" when Mommy wasn't looking.

"They'll wash off," I said, and proceeded with my grocery shopping.

Prayer:

Dear Lord, Let our past mistakes wash away too and not leave images to trouble us. Amen.

Fake It, Freddy

For even the son of man came not to be ministered unto, but to minister, and to give his life a ransom for many.

Mark 10:45

For a final project in the home economics exploratory class, the children decided to make catnip mice to donate to the pound. The pound sells little handmade cat and dog toys for one dollar each and uses the money for supplies and other expenses. One day, as we were stitching away, Freddy said,

"We're putting the work into these mice. Why don't we get the money?"

Ah, Freddy. I want you to experience the joy of being selfless, the reward of devoting time, energy, and money to causes, the satisfaction of doing for those who can't help themselves, and to help end the senseless destruction of God's wonderful little creatures.

Freddy and I talked quietly in the hall. I explained my motives and told him, bluntly, that if he didn't agree, he could at least fake it in front of me.

Freddy pushed himself after that and turned out one more mouse than anybody else.

Good boy, Freddy!

Prayer:

Dear Lord, Help us to be more giving and forgiving. Amen.

Make Your Own Fun

> Not that I speak in respect of want: for I have learned, in whatsoever state I am, therewith to be content.
>
> Philippians 4:11

"I'm bored," groaned Alison the first week of summer vacation. My car was in the shop; Alison's best friend was out of town, and we were otherwise stranded at the trailer nursing Panda back to health after she was spayed.

"You sometimes have to make your own fun," I said. Alison is usually very good at entertaining herself, but I think all the circumstances tying us to our home were overwhelming her.

"Come here a minute," I said. "Look at this little dog."

Alison came and sat beside me on the couch. Panda, who never seemed to suffer any loss of energy or enthusiasm due to her surgery, had pulled one of my bunny rabbit slippers out of her toy box and was lying on the rug worrying it. As she vigorously shook it back and forth, she let it go, watched it sail into the air, and then pounced upon it. Again, she grabbed the slipper in her jaws, pointed her nose to the floor as she seriously worried the rabbit to and fro, then looked so surprised as her nose pointed skyward and that slipper just happened to sail away from her. Again she pounced. Panda kept this up for about twenty minutes in an area of about nine square feet in our small living room. She was totally oblivious to us and was having a grand old time.

Thank you for the good example, Panda. Thanks, not only for making your own fun, but also for entertaining Alison and me one week in June.

Prayer:
Dear Lord, Let us delight in the simple things in life. Amen.

They Can!

> But be ye doers of the word, and not hearers only, deceiving your own selves.
>
> James 1:22

At the time I am writing this last story, we are two weeks into a new school year. I am no longer the fifth grade teacher but have moved up with my fifth graders of last year to become the sixth grade math/science teacher.

We have already undertaken an aluminum can recycling drive this year. I remember how well my class did in the newspaper-recycling contest last year, and I had high hopes in the can venture.

A bag or two of cans trickled in from my sixth graders, plus two of my students undertook the task of collecting juice cans that were discarded daily in the school waste baskets. A few bags came in from the seventh and eighth graders.

On the last morning of the can drive, there was a knock on my classroom door. It was the new fifth grade teacher.

"Got some cans for you!" she said. "Can you come downstairs for a moment?"

When I stepped outside the school, there was a father with his fifth grade son, standing behind a large pickup truck, its bed filled with garbage bags.

"Where do you want 'em?" the father asked.

"Are those all cans?" I asked.

The father nodded.

"Fantastic!" I said. "Let's put them in the grass in front of my car."

We counted fifteen heavily laden garbage bags of aluminum cans. Father and son beamed as I expressed my gratitude and surprise.

"Add these to the pile," said a voice. I turned to see the fifth grade teacher again. She threw several more bags of cans onto the grass.

"All from the fifth grade?" I asked.

She nodded.

It took me three days to get all the fifth grade cans to Charleston in my little Subaru. This morning at the recycling center we weighed in at 198 pounds of aluminum cans, and I accepted $75.44 for the school.

The fifth grade has again proven themselves as responsive, dependable, and selfless little beings. I had offered a ten-dollar first prize to the one who brought in the most cans and a five dollar second prize, but many of the children did not even count their cans. They just wanted to contribute to the cause. The fifth grade boy who had brought in over thirty dollars worth of cans with his father's help was tickled just to get his ten-dollar first prize.

The ten/eleven year olds have shown me again that they are willing to expend effort and energy to do things to make the world a better place.

God bless you, fifth graders.

Our Heavenly Father:
Help us to see the good qualities in all children no matter their age. Also, help us make the world a better place for our beloved canine friends. Amen.